THE CATCHER'S DREAMS

by

Warren Petoskey

Copyright © 2024 Warren Petoskey

All rights reserved. No part of this publication may be reproduced, distributed, or transmitted in any form or by any means

ISBN:

979-8-321960-16-5 (Paperback)

979-8-321960-34-9 (Hardback)

Introduction

The Catcher's Dreams

Poetry by Warren D. Petoskey

I remember being lost with no life reference. I started writing my thoughts. I share them cautiously because, to me, it is like baring one's innermost self, but also to realize if we are to progress in our walk with the Lord, honesty is the only policy and possibly that the poetry expressions might help someone else.

A few months ago, my wife went through my files and desk and found bits and pieces of the poetry I have written over the years. She piled all this paper in front of my computer and told me that I needed to get it all into a manuscript. I am nearly finished with this effort.

While compiling and writing the manuscript, the piece below came to me after reading and posting a number of pieces of poetry. Now, whether it is poetry or not is up to whoever reads it.

I did share this piece of my poetry with an elder friend who said, "Don't change one word!" So, I decided this piece should be the inaugural effort announcing this book containing my poetry, which I have entitled *Reflections of My Heart*.

Dedication

I may not have considered this manuscript if it had not been for my wife prodding me. My wife calls it poetry, but that identity belongs to the reader. I wrote these pieces over several years more as therapy than anything else.

So, I asked my wife, Barb, to write a review now and here it is:

Barbara Louise Curton Petoskey

"My husband has honored me by asking me to write a review regarding his poetry book entitled, "Reflections of My Life." This is a book I have been anticipating for over 50 years that is some reflection of our 56-year journey together.

We met in a small farming community in southeastern Michigan. I was 15 years of age and he was 21. He had just moved back to the community where I had been living in Illinois.

I had never met anyone like him. He loved the out-of-doors and, like me, he found beauty in songs and "magic" in music's timeless simplicity.

During our courtship, he would recite poems from great poets and play Johnny Cash ballads on his guitar. He won my heart! He often quoted the poem to me entitled, "How Do I Love Thee!"

Because of the difference in our ages, I was cautious about our relationship and his attention at first, but he won my heart.

Throughout our marriage, he has written his dreams, passions and accomplishments in poetry on scraps of paper he hid away in his file cabinet.

I feel these pieces of poetry he has written over 50 years will be enjoyed by many. His poetry will present messages inspiring hope, laughter and maybe some tears as well.

These pieces of poetry are reflections of where he was in the moment and my husband's ultimate commitment to The Creator of Life!"

Thank you, My Love

Looking back, my effort at writing poetry was and is therapeutic.

Contents

The Authentic Self	7
Our Garden	10
What I Will Do	12
Shadowed Reflections of Stockbridge, Michigan	13
Remembering Grandpa	18
Winter Speaks	19
The Living's Soul	20
A Day of Anxiety	21
In Memory of My Friend	22
Inspiration	23
Pondering	24
On Eagles	26
Human Estate	27
Still Friends	28
No Music	29
A Distant Land	30
The Tigress	31
The Founder's Day Parade	32
A Generation Awaits	33
The Final Solution	34
Thoughts of Spring	35
Sweetest Day	36
Confusion Faded	37
The Vietnam Veteran Dead	38
A Warm, Soft Summer's Night	40
Rise of a Stormy Wind	41
Angel's Unaware	42
Swan Road – Grandpa's Farm	44
Endtime	49
A Prayer	50
Too Bad	51
Words of A Native Son	53
I Met The Master Face-to-Face	55
Clouds	56
A Life In Progress	57
Thinking of My Wife	58
The Lights of That City	59
Little Girls	60
The Arrival, I Think	61
Life Traveler	63
Honoring Arnold and Margaret	64
I AM	65
In New Mexico	66
My Summit of Life	67
Aging Poem, I have wanted to write:	68

Lake Superior	69
When They Look at Me	71
The Road	73
Sites Past	75
In Pursuit of Purpose	76
When The Roses No Longer Bloom	77
Reflections	78

I add this recent piece as part of my introduction:

The Authentic Self

Who am I, I ask
My masks moving
Layers I've accrued
In my coverup
In my makeup
What will uncover
As I recover
Will I believe
Or fall apart
The looks, like this
Aged and gray-headed
All the disguises gone
My emaciated body
Hanging on bones
Smiling in pain
Hoping for renewal
Of some youth restored
Trying to recall
Looking deep into
My foggy memory
What I think I lost
I can't seem to remember
What it is and who I lost
Seems so long ago
Maybe another world
Possibly another place
Peering in waning sight
Maybe just another life

A thought, a dream
I wander now
To find the authentic me
I am not sure you see
I really can't see me
The dreamer and visionary

I think I used to be
But now feeling a poser
An imposter
Crippled of mind
But not of heart
In times past
Trying to access expectations
Wondering what mask fits today
This hour and place I am in
Hoping one will be right
My efforts seem futile
In a constantly moving pace
Efforts searching though adrift
The seas around me raging
Me trying to be calm
But a panic rising
Oh, the lost unfound
Me, and the unfinished work
The authentic me
The man buried in a shallow grave
Years of carnal abuse and refuse
My own creations and others assuaged
At times hearing an irregular heart-beat
Muffled by years of sinking sand
Life sometimes in bland colors
Keys sounded of senselessness
Played to a symphonic cacophony
That makes no sense
Yet, there is always the beat
And me moving my feet
Neon lights blinking in the street
Courage at one time

Came from a bottle
Buried in the myth
Blinding me from what I might see
Transportation to the place where
I don't know me and I am happy
But always the hangovers

And with sobriety
The never-ending question
The image in the mirror asks
Who is that staring back at me
I know I am lost somewhere
In the hues behind façade of parade
I had to go to my Shrink
He has nail scars in His hands
And a hole in His side
He is my Creator and I am told
He made me
So He should know
Who I am and what I could be
I think to myself
There is a He
Save me from dementia, I cry
Deliver me from this dark place
I called from my deep abyss

Save me please
Am I too blind to see
And then suddenly
In my own upper room
Hands reached down
Lifting me free
From a hellish grave
Into a marvelous light
I had never seen
But now for the first time
And through His effort
The blinders removed
The refuse relieved
I can see for the first time
I feel like Paul
My own Road to Damascus
To discover the authentic me
He birthed me to be!

Our Garden

There are times I grieve over the past we once knew
The invaders called this continent a wilderness
But we knew this place as a garden
At least that is what I was told
But I am reminded now
To no longer look backward
To focus on where I am going
Enough has happened to me
Since I was a young boy
That inspires me to believe there is a paradise
That awaits my arrival
I am at this stage of my life
Having developed from spiritual infancy
Growing in my understanding and focus
As an elder among our people, I write such things
To remind all of us human beings
That long ago, all of us had this consciousness
I am not grieving so much for what I have lost
But rejoicing over what I have found
I purchased the treasure in a field
In the midst of the pollution abounding
And gained more than I could have dreamed
So I walk this walk and talk this talk
My memory of the past reminds me of who I am
Not what might have been
The invaders' way has no evidence of better
Proven by all the decadence promoted
Far worse than what my ancients knew
And so I speak now in this way
When the invaders came, they pointed to a book
To identify who they are and justify what they did
I have read their book and find them not true
And the god they claimed to serve falsely presented
When we became destitute enough and powerless
We turned to pray and fast
The God you claimed appeared to us

And pointed to His Way away from what was forced on us
So now I live dying knowing at my death
I will inherit eternal life
I did not meet this Great One in a church
But in desperation, running to hide
And He appeared at my side
A vision, a dream but in a moment's time
He appeared as The One called Jesus
Some might argue though they weren't there
Now me knowing you cannot kill a dream like mine
I am reminded now what does it profit a man
If he gain the whole world but lose his own soul!

What I Will Do

The Elder told me,
"When you were young,
Like young people do.
You dressed yourself
And went where you
Wanted to!

Now that you are old,
Another will clothe you
And you will go
To places foreign
And you won't know.
You can trust Me though!"

"Faith will show you
What you don't know!
Remember what I saved you from
And the pit I found you in
Your blindness
And sickness because of sin!"

"You were rejected
And ridiculed by men
A glimmer of light
Brought you hope
You decided to pursued
Now freed from your plight."

"Remember that all I ask you to do
Is lead My people from their wrong to My right!
You have witnessed what I am about
Speak of My love and hope for them
By sharing what I have done
Promising them, "I will do for you!"

Shadowed Reflections of Stockbridge, Michigan
Sometime after 1990: driving through the country and town reviving boyhood memories:

I hesitate here and there in my memories quest
Down old sought-out shady lanes
Sun-baked houses and empty barns
Old landmarks now almost hidden
Me pulled about as I was bidden
Among now the shadowed reflections of my past

Ghostlike figures of old kind faces
Their hands raised to wave as I drive by
Long gone now I remind myself
Their aged voices I can hear still
Fragmented memories flood my mind
Of softer days and gentler ways

I wonder if like me others come
Who like me seek to find
Pausing in their moment of passion
Travelers too in their memories quest
Recovering fragments of years gone by
A reorientation as much at best

The little village no longer the same
Strangers present I never knew
I still recall the bellowing sound
Of old steam trains as they approach
John Deere tractors working the earth
Children playing about in their mirth

The memory appears of a boy of four
With a handful of pennies at Watkin's Store
Dad's Cadillac, a '38 Dodge appears
Memories of Sunday rides to Unadilla
Fights on the new TV at The Sweetshop
Friday nights filled in the wonderment

Pastures filled with Jersey cows
Cicada's buzzing in the trees
The Grainery nearby processing wheat
The smell of peppermint fills the air
New mown hay the odor I recall
Summers unparalleled I think

I hear Mom's concertos and sweet voice
Awakened by angelic sounds
The sun's rays expelling the dark
Dad's rich voice chiming in
I think no one richer than me
And then wonder what Heaven will be

The coolness of a summer evening
Barking dogs in the waning light
Skipper, The Wonder Dog, at my knee
The crickets begin their night's charade
Dad resting nearby in his chair
Another day heralded we all can share

Screen doors slamming shut down the street
One by one as families retreat
To the sanctity of their homes to sleep
Radios played to catch the evening news
Children tucked in beds to dream
Another day in a bit of paradise

An old schoolhouse with gilded halls
Children of all ages and classes met
Well-trimmed hedges protect the grass
Students running not to be late
Girls in saddle shoes holding books
Boys in U.S. Keds on the run

Across the tracks is the pickle mill
Cucumbers arriving there by crate
Men busy in the musky depths
Their processing secretly kept
Pungent dill around in the air

Delicious pickles out the other end
An old man comes to mind
Who shared his pickles at lunchtime

Grandpa Howlett comes before my eyes
I know! Long passed memories gentle and kind
The rides on Saturdays to the farm
In the charm of his old Model A
He smoking R.G. Dunn's on the way
The kind of joy that fills a boy's heart

Old Pat, the hunting dog, tied
In the midst of the chicken pen
Grandpa's chickens scratching the dirt
Time for crickets to be caught, I think
Sold at two cents apiece or more
Money for cold pop at a downtown store

Wheat harvest season now begins
Wagons pulled by tractors carrying loads
Orange and green tractors lined in a row
Pausing in their turn to shed their weight
Street lights revealing each tractor's place
Farmers visiting as they wait

Ballgames competitive in the vacant lot
Teams challenging each other with shouts
Donned in baseball hats and gloves
Opposites chosen on the spot
Eyeing each other before the game
Victory sought and the fame

On The Square in the center of town
Sits the only cinema known around
Saturday Matinee twenty-five cents each
My brother, sisters and I
Rushing down to the front
To see the real Tarzan on the screen

Outside Mr. Kitley's print shop
Where inside the printing presses click
The rhythmic beat, I can hear still
The printed work comes from the run
A fine edition every time
The paper called Stockbridge's Brief Sun

Across the tracks, the onion storage
Weekend bond-fires recalled outside
Musicians gathering in the fire's light
Old wooden crates chosen for chairs
The sound of guitars, banjos and fiddles rise
Singers accompanying blending in
Music arising for the soul

Andy Lindberg's fix-it shop
We gathered at the front window at 3 o'clock
A TV displaying looney tunes we watched
Laughing at the antics on the screen
Andy watching us in return
As we stood laughing at what we had seen

Orla Oakley's down the block
The first homespun TV I knew
The Lone Ranger came on the screen
Add to this Gunsmoke and Milton Berle
Their series continuously ran
And that glorious image of Superman

My heart jumped when I heard the words
My dad said when he declared on Saturday mornings
Let's go to Jone's Lake fishing son
A new Johnson reel and rod in my hands
We rented a boat at Beecham's house
Rushing I recall fish our quarry to take

Fresh milk Monday mornings on the porch
From Hickory Ridge Dairy outside of town
Glass bottles filled to the brim
Bearing the motto that we knew true

"Fresh as The Morning Dew
Direct from Farm to You!"

Fresh ground coffee from the general store
An old stetson cowboy comes into view
On horseback down the street
An unusual site here in The Mid-east
His name was Sam we found out
Revered by all who came to see

Potato bins and old ice chests
Ice brought in a horse-drawn wagon
An old, gray-bearded man in the driver's seat
Rose vines climbing trellises along a path
And gracing white picket fences as a treat

Goldfish in the pond out back
Currants blessings in brushy rows
Quail singing their poignant song
The neighbors waving with a smile
Magic days I could recall
Summers graduating into golden falls

You know it really seems
The girls were prettier then
I chose one to be my wife
Among the lilacs blooming red and white
You know, Sweetheart
It is still Me and You!

Remembering Grandpa

An old man in a porch swing
Early on a Sunday morn
Waiting for conversation, I think
I'll make time to sit awhile
Even though porch swings are not my style

We talked about small town things
As I sense the old man's genuineness
His easy manner putting me at rest
This old man on that porch swing
Back and forth in rhythm as the birds sing

The old man paused to listen now
Maybe a song I did not hear
The old man with his eyes shut
Listening as the music echoed in the summer air
I thought no other sound could be so fair

No other moment can I compare
To the old man sitting there
Reveling in the chorus that rang
He paying homage to the heavenly din
It seemed the birds were singing just for him

Fall 1991

Winter Speaks

A sense of coolness in the air
The summer trade winds turned anew
The leaves on the trees changing hue
Songs of geese in flight as they parade
Southward to a warmer place

Woodsmoke odor on the breeze
Leaves rustling as they fall
The earth hardens beneath my feet
A northeast winds reminding all
A dusting of early snow discreet

Woodpiles made grow cord upon cord
The corncribs filled to the eves
Garden plots turned and tilled
Ice forming on the lakes
And the air reminds one of the chill

Whitened silence every where
Stillness left the only sound
The earth rests blanketed deep
And creatures in their dens fast asleep
Winter speaks of a coming Spring.

The Living's Soul

I've been a long time getting here
So much detail to consider
All these along these weary treks
Many roadways still to map
Nothing sure or even pat
The fearful need not here appear
This road for those who ponder hope
The choices evident each long day
Honor The One who urged us here
Concrete structures reach the sky
But danger lurks in the alley ways
All travelers here we pray be aware
The neon lights and the trickery
The supreme court and religious edicts
In the dark warlocks and witches
Horror scopes a daily fare
Advertising promising care
Alcohol, crack cocaine and fentanol
Users needles litter the streets
Televisions constant dreg's morass
Children's minds the fertile ground
Nothing more damaging and profound
As spiritual darkness slowly creeps
Lulling listeners and benevolent to sleep
The watchers and prophets now bound
Peace and safety becomes our cry
While many around us slowly die
The plagues arise we suffer now
All because we will not allow
The life ring sent to rescue all.

1991
A Day of Anxiety

My cathedral is not fettered by man-made walls
It reaches far beyond the universe
Limited only by mortal thought
Science contemplates what God said true
Furrowed brows and questions wrought
Boundaries anew but limited still in kind
By the vanity of the limited human mind

Differences between this finite being
My attitude conveyed by level of flight
Humanity in his bigoted thought
Groping in the dark about destiny at hand
Unaware and indifferent to all
Unseeing the universe's promised end
And The Judge watching who sits in Hallowed Halls

Build your asphalt pleasures if you must
Memorials decaying declaring your view
Theology proposed without foundation
Disregarding The Stone the builders set at naught
And though your structures number many
Your unseeing statues with morbid faces
In ignorance of the building God wrought

Help me, Lord! On days like these
Remind me to see the pit from which I came
The pit still occupied by the world's masses
The prize awaits for me to claim
My labors here on earth remain
Nothing to hinder my walking on
Patiently, quietly in my current estate

In Memory of My Friend

Giants, my friends,
Among us stand
Though just men
Undeterred and unafraid
Faith personified
Displayed
Carrying Light
Boldly adorned
Carrying The Sword
The Word
Loving Righteousness
Preaching, living
Representing truth
The Truth
Salvation
The Gospel of Peace
He endured to the end
Strong, devout
Spiritual Man of God
Renowned Heroes identified
Powerful legacy
Warriors
The Beauty of God
Earthbound but Heaven seen
Free Humble
Epistles viewed and read
Of all men!

Inspiration

Inspiration comes and goes
I think sometimes I miss it though
Absorbed with this life's little cares
I am not always alert or seemingly aware.

As the years go by, I do find
Time does not pass slowly or kind
Now to the ancients, I am drawn
My youthful skills long gone.

There is a new effort to maintain
Attention given to love and peace
The blessings The Lord has freely given
I give as I am asked and bidden.

November 1, 1994. Thinking about some of the teachers I have been with, what they taught and how my life changed.

Pondering
Ponder with me awhile, if you will?
A day long ago and a lonely hill
Though far removed from history's halls
The scene dim to some, but not to all
A disfigured man and His sacrifice
Addressing the human estate with price
Paying the price for all who are lost
A reminder of the ghastly deed
The production of a vile heart's greed
This man guilty of only good
At the whipping post he withstood
A cruel lashing by a soldier's hand
Enduring the taunts of a vigilante crowd
Ushered on and their purpose set
Evidences of what evil begets
A scourging so vehemently foul
The high priests face a pious scowl
Requiring the man to carry his cross
Upon that cross a bleeding back
Through the ravenous crowd on a narrow street
To a particular place on Golgotha's Hill
He hung that day between heaven and hell
And when he passed a sense of dearth
Fell through the crowd quelling their mirth
Fear arose as the evening came
Darkness hovered over and the rocks rent
Even the ground heaved as all nature rebelled
Humans fleeing to their hovels to hide
Sober now from the carnage and feast
Consciences pricked conviction arises
But days have passed and consciences less
The price required was now paid
The body in fine linen was gently laid

In the sepulcher a rich man's grave
Women attending their vigil still
Their prayers echoing from the hill
In their tears an angel appears
He is not here and is risen today
Now to us two thousand years
Continues the approach this prophetic bier
Announcing the beginning of this church age
And soon to begin His millennial reign
He continues to be the only Door
Through which entry can be gained
The water and The Word the only Way!

2/20/90
On Eagles

I look at him through nurtured eyes
The airy heights where the eagle flies
My heart rising to meet the wind
I, listening, anticipating his cry
Urging me to climb with him
I, with these feigned wings and slim
Into these lofty halls of God

Little does my feathered friend
Consider the physical limits I am in
I wear their feathers in my hair
Acknowledging their regal and high estate
I honor his flight in his blue estate
Grounded here I know my place
But honoring the eagle in his flight of grace

April 23, 2023
Human Estate

When the roses no longer bloom
And the sun no longer shines
When the birds no longer sing
And love dies in the gloom

When light turns to darkness
And hope lies dying in the street
And the only peace is bought with guns
And truth falls at one's feet

And our Creator abandons the scene
Relief sought but without access
Baby's carcasses litter the land
And nothing left sacred or serene

Human beings in the wake
Not knowing the sarcophagus prepared
Is for each of them who emerge
And in the distance a funeral dirge

Like the lemming running to escape
Their drowning in the sea awaits
No one now to point the way
To the higher road that is straight

Ignore the obvious if you will
The subverted will soon find
That the life promised
But entrance now denied!

April 24, 2023
Still Friends

If I don't talk to you today
Please don't just go away
Before I get to talk to you again
You have always been my treasured friend
And we agreed because of the love
We would never be so far
Or too absent-minded
We couldn't recall
We have come some distance together
Traveling through this world below
To that promised place
We have heard and agreed to seek
Determined to earnestly contend
To pursue until our life path ends
If one of us is called earlier
We know we will meet again
On the other side
Sharing notes about where we've been
Reminded again we are still friends!

No Music

There is no music now
Just heartbeats
Echoing, breaking the silence
The darkness deepened
Penetrated only by a great Light
Conditions obvious it would seem
The Light of mercy shines so
The threat and fear
Forced to disappear
Death dismissed
Like an undisciplined child
We reminded of an empty grave
Kindness and love reappear
The Water, oh The Water
Hope fills the human atmosphere
Cups offered filled over-flowing
A feast prepared
In The Land promised
In the Dwelling God built
For those who will.

A Distant Land

I have not traveled here before
But I have listened to ancient lore
And now wondering if it's true
Will this ancient trail take me
From where I am to You.

I am traveling, really, from nothingness
Having heard of an ancient promise made
After You, Lord, suffered and arose from the dead
You left to prepare a place for us
That where you are we may be too!

I can see the path clearly ahead
Leading into the shadows of the trees
I know of no other way
For me to go in this dark day
As I continue my pursuit of a promise made!

Sorry friends but I have to leave
Drought has compelled me now to go
I hope you too, will join me soon
This place we are in shambles true
Living here now for me a struggle.

Alone I continue to step
Following this travel-worn ancient path
Believing in the promise that lies ahead
As far more comforting than I know
Escaping the emptiness evident here.

The Tigress

In the shadows of the darkened glen
Fierce eyes pierce the moonlit night
As a tigress searches for its prey
Ears straining for a desired sound
Of an anticipated feasts approach
The quickness of the cat invades the light
And in one single bound
Its quarry struggles
In the tigresses grip
She dragging the meal to a hidden lair
Two kittens anxiously appear
The tigress prepares and tears this prey
She had just caught Sustenance for days
Till when all that is left of the passing prey
Is washed away by the tigresses caress!

The Founder's Day Parade

A band playing a raucous, inebriated march
Gay colored banners and streamers flying
Lemonade stands a dime a glass
Decorated old wagons as floats roll by
Young ladies stride in lovely gowns
Town officials on pedestals where they pose
Waving at the crowds with frozen smiles
Looking for encouragement from the jubilant crowd
Children on rusty bicycles hurry on
With colored crepe paper and spoked playing cards
Clowns with bulbous noses and red hair
Walking on stilts with unrealistic big feet
The smell of cider and cotton candy waft by
Heralded the Founder's Parade on the Fourth of July!

A Generation Awaits

A generation waits for us today
For a message from the past to come
To lead the world out of the quandary where we reside
Defined by love lost and mindless things
Which bind us in this present time.

Life has a regal, treasured value
Fulfilled when we reach our grave
Is not measured by worldly gain
Nor the sensual memories we might retain
But rather have we given and loved enough.

We are but travelers passing through life
Into endless paths and corridors
Children mark our passage here
Life for them will be measured
By the legacy we dedicated

Ideas and systems come and go
But all that really matters now
Isn't the marble memorials we construct
But did we learn and live lessons well
The truth in our children's lives will tell!

7/10/92
The Final Solution

The stage is set
The actor's all in place
Infamy the play's title
Many awaiting the titled cue
Declared approaching with tinkling sounds
No meaning but deadly profound
Decadence there echoes and rebounds
Judgement at The Throne
And thus begins the final act
A new Director takes His place
Somber faces looks of humility appear
Beckoned into eternity to approach
And face our Father, The Judge of us all!

4/11/91

These days have been stressful, so I pictured fields full of flowers and this poem is the result.

Thoughts of Spring

April is here Spring flowers due
I, in anticipation
Of the green hues
The bright, colored splashes
Of reds, yellows and blues
A sun warmed earth
Fresh green grasses
This essence before unseen
My vision here inspired
Announcing this spring anew
"A blessing from God to you!"

1989
Sweetest Day

It is that time of year we designate,
To recognize our hearts' choice
That person with whom we spend our life
And now to whom I lift my voice.

To my Sweetheart these many years!
Every day begins anew!
Now, in quest for ways I might express
My admiration and love for you!

Somehow, words don't seem enough
When I think of all we have shared
My feeble attempt to say to you
To express how much I care.

My mind recalls the day so well
I saw a young woman walking down the street
The sunlight blessed upon her hair
I hurried a plan wanting to meet.

If you will remember, Love,
When I looked into your eyes and said,
"Would you marry me!"
And join me, our pathways share?"

Together now, these many years
Seven children born along the way.
Each day grows much sweeter, Dear.
Now inspiring this declaration on this Sweetest Day!"

Confusion Faded

I come away alone today,
Not knowing for sure what I've found.
History, like a ghost, has caught up to me,
As I discover origins of my ethnic background.
In my dreams I have heard muted sounds
Drum-beats and singer's voices call.
I hear words ringing in the wind
Elder's stories as they share their tales,
Which echo around me everywhere.
Compelled here I stand new vistas clear,
No longer am I lost and alone.
The ancient's children welcome me,
And the chronic fear I felt is gone.
Great Spirit has smiled on me,
In granting me access to His Light.
The darkness I knew no longer is,
The force that hinders me!

When will we ever get from the position of thinking we are Job's comforters to the place where we realize we are Job?

A Vietnam Veteran was found dead along a highway. He had passed out from being drunk and died of exposure beside the road. Of course, there were those who had no sympathy for the man or his death, but they had never considered the conditions this man was subjected to in combat and how difficult it is to get the nightmares that combat projected out of one's head.

This poem is a reflection of my feelings and prayer:

The Vietnam Veteran Dead

I have something to tell you, my friends,
I wonder if this is where you fit in,
This is about a man found today,
Along the course of a two-lane highway.

No one came to claim his remains,
No one to take his body home.
He died in a country, rural place,
Drunk and all alone.

He was someone's long, lost brother,
He surely was someone's son,
But when they asked for family,
There seemed to be no one!

The dog tags that hung around his neck,
Revealed who he was and where he had been,
And it was found he was
A decorated combat soldier in Vietnam,

The ceremony for him was not regal,
No mourners came to mourn or weep,
No flowers circled his pauper's casket,
No one besides we who knew.

You won't find his name in stone engraved,
Among the memorials honoring Vets at Arlington.

But it really doesn't make any difference now.
He is listed by us as a Vietnam Combat Vet anyhow.

February 7, 1992
A Warm, Soft Summer's Night

Warm and soft summer nights
Croaking frogs and fire flies
Crickets singing in harmony
Leaves whispering in the trees
The smell of dew on earthen moors
The greeting of a great horned owl
The closing of an old screen door
The squeak of a rocking chair
In the distance a dog barks
I hear "Amen!" to a child's prayer
Voices fading with the light
Some of the old lovely sounds
On a warm and soft summer's night.

September 1992
Rise of a Stormy Wind

Today a fierce wind drifted here
The petals from the flowers quickly fell
Forced from by the cold, gusting breeze
With the wind came an eerie chill
Reminding us a season is giving way
Further evidenced by fall colors start on the hill
Flocks of summer birds are in the air
Riding the north wind to places fair
The cold messaging like a trumpet's blast
Reminding the beholder to prepare
The staging for winter is set and cast.

After hearing the story of a young boy's drowning and then hearing the rest of his story:

Angel's Unaware

There were trailers on the old camp grounds
Children laughing and playing on the swings
People milling all around
A little boy with tousled hair
Came forward hands buried in pockets deep
He seemed to appear out of nowhere
A cotton shirt one button at the top
Bib overalls, no shoes or socks
That night after the preacher's words
The boy came to the preachers back
Tugged on his coat afterwards
"I heard your message and I want so much
To come here all the time to hear?"
Looking down, the boy said,
"I got better clothes and shoes
Do you suppose it would be all right?
Can I come again tomorrow night?"
The preacher's eyes looked down to see
The boy who stood at his knee
He could not resist telling him
"You have found a Friend here tonight.
That One they call The Great Light!
You are welcome here anytime!
Don't you worry about what you wear
To all of us you look just fine!"
The following night during the offerings call
The preacher looked to see the boy
Walking up the aisle straight and tall
And in his hand a single rose
"I knew you took up offering!" He said
"I prayed for something I could give
Along the way a bird took wing
From a bush I saw

Where this flower appeared so beautiful
And I picked it knowing it was for you!"

The morning came with the sorrowful news
Concerning the little blond-haired boy
Had fallen into a watery pit
Where he lost his life
The reason why remains unknown
But The Scripture comforts all who ask
The Lord would make the bad for good
When the preacher made the altar call
The boy's mom and dad appeared

One small boy whose faith stood out
Just a cotton shirt one button at the top
Bib overalls no shoes or socks
A single rose from a bush unseen
The Scripture and the preachers call
To gentle hearts pure and clean
The Presence of The Will of God
Few before had seemed to care
For some it seems we entertain
The presence of Angel's unaware!

2/20/91
February, but little snow. After driving through the country near my grandfather's farm:

Swan Road – Grandpa's Farm

I hesitate in a memory's quest
Down old shady lanes
Sun-dried farms and hills
Old landmarks now almost hidden
Me pulled along as I am bidden
Shadowed reflections recalled at best

I think of old, kind faces passed
Hands wave in friendly jests
The cherub faces of yesteryears
Aged voices carried upon the wind
Fragments come of events gone by
And me remembering to make them last

The little town where I grew
The traveled streets I once knew
Steam train's whistles echo on
In the outskirts rolling fields
John Deere's bellow plowing the earth
Children playing in the park's shield

A boy of four at the candy store
Dad's black 38' Dodge
I thought the greatest car of all
The fights broadcast on Friday nights
Gillette and TV in The Sweet Shop
Pastures filled with milking cows

Cicada's buzzing from the trees
The sounds raised from the grainery
The smell of peppermint in the air
The sirens of the fire trucks
Summer's cadence rich and fair
Mom's piano and sweet voice

In the early morning light
Sounds ushered in the early morning air
Dad's voice deep and strong
Melodies sang as he joined in
And me thinking how rich I am
Now recalling the front porch set

Barking dogs and waning light
Skipper resting at my feet
Comforting to me the day complete
Dad nearby reading his paper
While leaning back in his porch chair
And screen doors closing up the street

One by one families retreat
Into their homes sleepy light
The smell of coffee freshly brewed
Radios now sounding
Promoting the evening news
Children made to wash their feet

The old schoolhouse and playground
Where all ages and classes met
Fine trimmed hedges protect the school's grass
Students arrive with books in tow
New saddle shoes climb the steps
Conversing with friends as they go

The summer's visit, I recall to a factory
Where cucumbers turned to pickles
Men working in the musky depths
Their activities secretly kept
Pungent smell of dill in the air
Jars of pickles out the other end

Grandpa comes before my eyes
Though long passed from this life
Recalling his old Ford Model A
His chickens scratching in the dirt

Saturday trips out to this farm
Remembering the smell of his cigars

Crickets I caught and sold
My prices raised to two cents each
Old Spike Tisch bought them all
I continued hunting them under rocks
Hoping to find many to catch
Thinking of ice cream and a cold pop

Wheat harvesting season soon begins
Wagons burdened and being towed
By orange, red and green tractors fine
Waiting their turn in line
Dispensing into the boxcars what they reaped
Endless it seemed each successive night

Ball games in the vacant lot
Challenging voices raised in support
Baseball hats, bats and gloves
Opposing teams chosen on the spot
Now facing off and initiating play
We felt, World Series here today!

On the square in the middle of town
The cinema with sidewalks around
Saturday matinee twenty-five cents
My brother, sisters and I
Pressing downward to the front
To watch Tarzan and Jane upon the screen

Across the square, Mr. Kitley's place
And hearing the printing presses noisily race
Their rhythmic beat I recall still
A newspaper appeared along the away
A fine edition every time
Called "The Brief Sun" by name

The nearby old onion storage
Recalling bond fires weekend nights

Musicians gather in the flickering light
Old wooden stumps gathered for chairs
Guitars, fiddles, banjos and bows
Producing music good for the soul

Andy Lindberg's fix-it shop
Where we kids gathered at three o'clock
Andy allowed us to come and stand
Outside the picture window in front
To watch cartoons on a television displayed
Awed and laughing, it was so much fun

My heart still remembers what my dad would say
"Let's go fishing, boy's, it's Saturday!"
New Johnson rods and reels to try
A rented boat at Jone's Lake
Oaring the boat I recall well
Fish waiting our quarry to take

Fresh milk on the porch each morning too
Fresh from the dairy at Hickory Ridge
Delivered promptly at our back door
Glass bottles with their motto displayed
"Fresh as the morning dew!
Direct from the farm To you!"

Justices of the peace upheld the law
Fresh ground coffee from the general store
An old stetson cowboy coming down the street
A pretty, big, palomino horse he rode
Unusual to some here in the Middle East
But Old Sam waved kindly, quietly discreet

Potato bins and old ice boxes
In horse-drawn carts the ice came
The gray-bearded man in the driver's seat
Rose studded trellis along the path
Goldfish and frogs in the fishpond
Apple and cherry trees blooming beyond

You know it seemed
The girls were all pretty back then
I decided to marry one of them
In June, the right season with the lilacs in bloom
Now many years later
Sweetheart, It still is me and you!

9/16/90
Endtime

Prophecy now unfolds
Messages remain unheard untold
Day, month and year convey
What most of the populace really fears
Running here and there, but nowhere
Churches bleached, dead and cold
Members fade and decease
People ill and not at ease
A foreboding feeling in the air
Oppression it seems everywhere
Looking to Armageddon
Without seeing the feast prepared
Truth awaits those who dare
Offering each The Way of escape
Predestination by authorization
Only to those who will believe
That the lost can be found
Fellowship and the breaking of bread
For those hungering for The King of all!

A Prayer

O God, my Spirit Chief, to you I call
From my meek, lowly estate here below
Lift me up above this rancor and pall
Promote me, Lord, to Your place of peace
Your blessings upon my wretched life bestow
Free me from my sin I pray
From this bondage and utter strife
Let me walk if I may
On that path You travel now
Above this stench and decadent decay

Jesus! I am an Indian man
You have inspired these many years
Let me speak if I can
Above the damage and Satan's scam
Tell of that glorious place
Prepared for those who will seek
Your Will to run this race
Remaining humble, in subjection and filth free
Believing The Truth above any lie
The only freedom here offered to live by

Too Bad

That you never got to ride in a Model A
Ever used an outhouse
Baled hay and stacked it in the barn
On a hot, muggy day
Fed the chickens or milked the cows
Ate homemade ice cream from a churn
Planted flowers in particular places
Fed the birds and the wild deer
And shocked corn and shelled it for feed
Ever woke up to the sound of music
Or read The Bible at least once
Done piece work in a factory all-day
Work ethic compelled by needs at home
Or gone hungry or been lonely
Do you know what life is like without TV
Made it your practice to listen more than you talked
Heard rooster pheasants crowing at morning's light
Heard a thousand crickets chirping all through the night
Whipporwill's warming night-pall
Or listened to a loon's call afar-off in the fall
Plowed and planted a garden by hand
Square - danced with a pretty girl to a barker's call
Did I mention riding in a Model A
Loved someone so much
The thought brought tears
Given money to someone in need because you could
Have you read Poe, Sandburg, Whitman or Frost
Slept in the woods all night just to listen to the night sounds
Worked a thousand-piece crossword puzzle to its end
And found out you could
Ate homemade bread your mother made
Topped with homemade butter or marmalade
Caulked and painted your grandpa's homemade boat
Fished in an ice shanty warmed by a kerosene heater
Played kick the can or pom-pom poll away
Do you remember your first kiss

Walked barefoot in the grass
Or seen a baby born
And because you did reverence life more
Remember the smell of new-mown hay
Or shoveled snow the old way
Ridden a beautiful quarter horse
Or heard the train whistle coming down the track
Swam jungle style in a private lake
Or had a Boston cooler at Watson's store on a hot day
Or worked for your grandparents because of need
Experienced the passing of a loved one
Mother and Dad wondered if you could keep breathing
Or reunited with a long-lost friend
Or sought forgiveness for your sins
The pickle factory and the old man
Or Cowboy Sam when he rode his horse
When all the streets in town weren't paved
And you shared a bed with your brother
Or ate beef tongue and glad to get it
Did you meet Old Spike Tisch
Or my Grandpa Howlett a pillar in our village
Or attended a pow-wow for impressions of a deeper life
Shared a home with a loving wife
Met Kaye Poe or her brother Bob
But then I think you have memories too
Of days gone by and those you knew
Aging dictates the day and though slower now
Jewels heralded along the way
Thankful another sunrise has come
Seventy-eight years have passed
Children with children now on their own
I think to remind them again of the love I have
For each of them
And thank my God, I am still here.

Words of A Native Son

I am a Native son and no stranger here
I come from a place called Crooked Tree
I've sat on a rock where my grandfather did
I like the feel of cool grass under my feet
I've watched flowers bloom and children born
I have studied the ants and the clouds going by
I have sat in the dark listening to the whippoorwills
Marveled at the colors the trees display in the fall
I have seen kittens born
I love a woman and she me
We slow dance to music most can't hear
I have been rejected by some and loved by others
I have experienced the bad and strive for the good
I have sat on the shore of Lake Superior in a storm
I have felt a good fish on a rod and line
I have tasted venison I harvested myself
I have sat and watched deer pass below
I have enjoyed holding a child's hand in mine
I have experienced meeting The Lord for the first time
I have danced in gatherings heralded by drums
I honor the elders and veteran's I'm among
I I know the healing touch of a mother's hand
I took joy in hugging my dad's neck
I have sung with a choir to a gospel song
I have often been moved by the preacher's call
I think as King David wrote, "Surely goodness and mercy!
Shall follow me all the day's of my life!"
I have hit a homerun that won the game
I am blessed everyday with good friends
I like the feel of snow in my face
I have enjoyed the solace of fishing on Lake Superior's ice
I like the sound of a beagle chasing a hare
I have hunted partridge over a good bird dog
I have climbed mountains and experienced the valleys
I still fear no evil knowing who protects me

I know a pastor who is my good friend
I have labored in prayer in the night season
I know the inspiration that comes through The Holy Spirit
I have enjoyed my guitar and me singing old songs
I have driven through a blizzard on a dark night
I have sat near a waterfall and felt the spray
I've caught smelt in the river with bare hands
I love frybread and fresh corn I shared
I married the woman of my dreams
I have drank cold water from mountain streams
My daughters and sons do love me
I know God has put me on a mission to complete
I am a trusted heir to His eternity
I am living and enjoying a good life!

I Met The Master Face-to-Face

I had walked life in a worldly way
Wherever pleasures and lust it seemed led
Until one troubled day to a quiet place
I met The Master face-to-face

Til then, status and wealth was my goal
Thought for my body and not for my soul
I was running in the world's maddening race
When I met The Master face-to-face

I met Him and sorrow met me
His eyes filled with sorrow I did see
I faltered and fell at His feet that day
My worldly castles vanished away

In their space a great new place
The Master's face I could plainly see
I bowed and cried, "Make me loving and meek!"
Allow me to walk in the steps of Your wounded feet!"

My thoughts are now for the souls of men
I lost my life only to find it again
Since that day in a quiet place
I met The Master face-to-face!

October 30th, 1985
Clouds

Where do clouds go?
Skipping across an azure sky
Hurrying along their way
To some unknown destination only they know?
Where do clouds come from?
And where do they go?
Rolling and growing
Reflecting the sky colors
Inspired by a bright sun
Smiling at me, but urging on..
Who can know Where they go?

A Life In Progress

There are times when I don't know what to say
I have found after years of trial and error
I am reminded that there is only one way
The trail that was broken by One who cares

I was inspired by what I didn't know
To leave my isle of ease discreet
And take that path less traveled by
Following a path blazed for me!

Thinking of My Wife

I quickly recall the day,
When I first saw you passing by.
And could not wait to see you again
Face-to-face and ask you why?

How had I missed you these many years?
How could you have been right here!
And me never noticing you before?
A treasure I love and long searched for.

Now, thank God, never apart
Since that day you said, "I do!"
The memories we have encountered
Give strong reason to why I love you!

August 17, 2023
The Lights of That City

There are times when I don't know what to say
I have found after years of trial and error
Reminded that there is only one way
The trail broken by One who cares

I was inspired by what I didn't know
To leave my isle of ease discreet
And take that trail less traveled by
Following a path blazed for me!

My promised land
Not far ahead now
Sometimes I think I see
That City's lights!

Remembering finding two graves in The Huron-Manistee Forest near Luzerne, Michigan:

Little Girls

I came upon two gravesites early today
In The Huron Forest these children lay
I can't help but wonder who takes care
Of these babies graves sleeping here
Few people pass this secluded site
There are wood picket fences painted white
Two headstones mark the mounds
Where these children lay and the only sounds
Come from the songbirds perched near
I wonder how many ever pause to see
Who these babies are resting here!

The Arrival, I Think

I've been a long time getting here
So much information to consider
Some treadmill years
So many roadways to map
Deceptions rampant everywhere
The world around me in discord
The fearful do not appear
Only those who ponder
Choices offered everyday
Being honest one must wonder
What delusions offered the devil's way?
Concrete structures in high rises
Danger lurking among the crevices
Travelers be alert and aware
The neon lights with crucifixes displayed
The supreme court and religious filets
Ladies of the night and even witches
Horror scopes present a daily fare
Labeling and advertising
Alcohol, meth, weed and crack cocaine
Users needles can declare
Televisions constant messages
Children's minds the fertile ground
Programs mental, soft massaging
Much shocking and too profound
Lulled again into sleepless nights
Hoping darkness will safely keep
The watchers and prophets chained
Yet Goliaths slain with little stones
Peace and safety here the cry
The echoing of fearful tones
The unaware and slowly die
Eating meat and breaking bread
Aids and covid suffered now
Eternity just up the road ahead

Sins stand out in scarlet red
But some disappear in the white snow
Wisdom beckons along the path
Reminding us all
Only what is done for Christ will last!

Life Traveler

I am an adventurer
I long to see what lies on the other side
Breathe the fresh air
Drink from the mountain streams
Hear The Creator's choirs enjoined when the bird's sing
Symphony's unmatched carried on the wind
I love the thrill of another sunrise and sunset
I walk with the elk among the lodgepole pine
I am the cougar looking down from atop cliff walls
I am the bald eagle and the hawk
Soaring through heaven's heights
The lithe falcon diving fast in flight
I am the grizzly who challenges all
I am the Odawa, Bodewattimi and Chippewa
I am the wind and the clouds
I am in the snow, hail and the rain
I am the cool earth soothing bare feet
I am the cold stream offering the water to bathe
I walk through the valleys to the mountaintops
I am the blue waters seen where fish abound
The sky is my cathedral and the earth my throne
I am God and God alone!

Honoring Arnold and Margaret

The fall and a quiet dirge
The glow a sacred fire lit
Wailing sounds in the dark
Two hearts gone from our midst
Their victories won
Two spirits free
No longer bound
Run on, I say
While I envy you
And grieve as well too
Memories fond I embrace
But continue on
To run my race
The battle calls
A warrior true
Compel me forth
In the smoke
But now for a moment
I pause and thank you both!

1/25/90

I wrote this after some prayer and meditation, expressing some concerns I had to The Lord. I feel this is how The Lord responded to me. Poetry? I don't know, but you can decide.

I AM

When the sun shines or in the storms, you can see Me.
When the rain falls, you will know it is I.
When it seems darkness surrounds you,
My Light will still be evident.
When each blessing comes
You will know it is a gift from Me.
With each chastisement you will sense My Love.
You are My child!
I am in the wind and the storm!
I speak and My Voice echoes throughout the world.
Where I stand, no one can fall.
I know every flower when it blooms.
I count the leaves because the trees are mine!
The winds from the East push the clouds across the sky,
I know where the clouds go!
I hear the voices of all of your children!
I see every smile and I hear every cry!
I still am Lord of Lords!
My Hand is stretched out still!
If you are hungry, I will feed you.
I will always be your friend.
Do not forget!
I know The Universe!
For it is Mine!
On a clear night or in the storm!
You can still see My Face!
I love you with a love that is hard for you to comprehend!
Seek Me!
Call out My Name and I will respond!

In New Mexico

I looked out through a purple-tinted haze
Towards the jagged mountains far away.
The promised rising of a bright, yellow sun
Heralding yet, another promised western day.
There on a distant cactus-dotted ridge
Stood an elder with feathers in his hair.
I could hear the drums rising thunder
The noise rose and fell with the air
A great, dark-colored beast, the first of many
Broke over the far sunlit rim.
A cloud of dust arose and followed
These buffalo crossing in this place
I climbed to view from a lofty point,
And as far as my eyes could see
These buffalo hurrying to a distant space.
My heart swelled at the bounty I saw
The Creator allowed me to see this day
I think I hear aged voices!
An echo of songs, worship here
The drums and rhythmic bells in time.
Maybe a dream or vision I don't know
Reminding me of who and whose I am
While I travel this Red Road!

My Summit of Life

I am rising towards the summit of my life,
From where I now stand reviewing life.
My destination almost in sight.
My path now not as long as before,
As it was when I started this way.
Aging approves my hair
And upon the wrinkles on my face.
My steps slower, but more sure,
I long to see the view from the top
I know there is no stopping here.
I have known victories and defeats
My eyes no longer clouded by my past,
The cares of this world, I know, don't last.
I think of my relatives on the other side
And My Precious Creator who patiently waits.

Aging Poem, I have wanted to write:

I am observant, as possible at seventy-five
The back of my hands are my litmus measure
And now look at hands completely foreign to me
The memory quickly arises of my grandpa's days
When he had arrived at this same place.

Wrinkled and dry without lotion applied
Arthritic and shaky no matter the chore
Dressing and brushing teeth more difficult than before
And when was it? I cannot recall
When I was so difficult to walk.

Days come and days go by
Too quickly the years now seem to fly
Tomorrow seems already yesterday
And no matter what my mind might try to say
The few who know are the ones who relate.

Loneliness now, more my friends
My age seems a barrier to the young
Now tired of the stories I still recall
And tell to anyone who will
Repeatedly, over and over again.

I remember when our babies grew up and left home
Mom and I had to adjust to the absence of the youth
The raucous busy noise abated in our home
Quietness sadly growing day by day
As I continue to make my way.
I still sing, "Take this whole world but give me Jesus!"
He remains all my hope and stay
Still, rejoicing over the day I at an altar prayed
He came to free me from my ghostly chains
He filled me with His Spirit and led me away.

I wrote this after returning to our home in Baraga, Michigan. Nearing the bay before the City of Marquette late at night the lake appeared like a glassy mirror. The reflections of the lights of the city spread towards me. I thought, "How beautiful!" but then remembered the story of Edmund Fitzgerald and many other stories of mariners and fishermen who lost their lives in the lake. I also remembered that the lake is so cold that it takes a long time for a human body in the depths to decay. While the scene evident was beautiful I knew it had a sinister side to it. I believe the year was 1979.

Lake Superior

A lady cradled by earthen bounds
A seductress held by bastions sound
She whispers with her temptress's voice
Dressed alluringly in colors most choice

She motions to the mariners in port
"Come sail into my concourse!"
Beguiling words of love proclaimed
Unseen in her grasp the rattle of chains

Soft swells beguiling the more
Enamored seamen ease from shore
Rising and falling on each wave's breath
Chided on by the undulous stretch

Of promising blue-covered peaceful depths
She entices other men to come
No clouds about, a sailor's sun
Serenaded by her perfumed caress

She readily dulling unconsciousness
She beckons the wind while the mariner sleeps
Urging it on to rise and sweep
The seafarer's senses dulled to the shift

A full "nor-easter" approaches swift
At first alarm, the craft swings about
As the waves rise with a raucous shout

In the distance, a crescendoing roar

Announcing waves rising the more
An attempt for safety on an ill-fated date
These hapless men join others in state
Who fell to this temptress's lure and behest

Her icy fingers, robbing their breath
The bells at the point toll again, as before
Her fury ebbed and calm restored
She reclines to her former estate

Beckoning others out for a date
More mariners ashore to embrace
She offers her soft, elegant charm
A sly smile colors her face

Alluring eyes wink the more
She calls again from her portal doors
Her perfume carried by gentle winds
Offering more than just an embrace
Luring more mariner's asea from shore.

(Footnote: this poem is part of a display at The Presque Isle Maritime Museum north of Marquette, Michigan.)

2016
When They Look at Me

What do people see when they look at me
My long gray hair, faltering steps and shaky hands
An old man, archaic and wandering
Slow in speech but long in talk with stories to tell
A rugged life that somehow turned out well

What do people see when they look at me
Can they see where I have been
Can they begin to comprehend the life I have lived
Scarred by struggle, determined to a certain end
The life I gave for the life I live

What do people see when they look at me
An Indian, activist, and watchman on the walls
Or just an ancient trying to stand tall
Looking off in some great vision
And taking a path prepared for me

What do people see when they look at me
A dreamer, dancer, and walking stick maker
A philosopher, writer, or wannabe
Unshackled and yet bound by an ethereal being
Moving always moving convincingly

What do people see when they look at me
A father, son, uncle, brother or friend
Or threat with motives undefined
Mysterious and out-of-line
With social motions or the economy

What do people see when they look at me
I am not as I once was
Time has worn away the shell
My feeble ability now betrayed
In the way, my actions are conveyed

What do people see when they look at me
Am I measured by what I say or don't say
Am I judged by the things I do or don't do
Am I dismissed because of the color of my skin
I can only be who I am.
What do people see when they see me!

The Road

The roads are open to all who travel
One leads to Heaven
All others lead to hell
Some lead to blessing
All others once traveled
Wring one out and cast a spell
The weary traveler addicted
Races against the darkness
Faster on a dead-end street
Oblivious to the loud signs
This road leads to hell
Warnings do not penetrate
Youthful lust and dangerous intent
Lives lost and ill-spent
Despite old travelers' weak attempts
Advice wasted what he or she knows?
Though traveled these roads before
Surviving the perils along the way

The ignorance now too evident
Others traveled that road before
Disappearing into the black abyss
Most roads tempt and implore
Glamor gained and bravery feigned
Born on the untried wings
"Don't take that road!"
Is the elder's cry, "sinkholes await!"
I traveled it and survived
There is a better-proven Way
Well-marked and full of Light
Without fear or stress or fright
A destination tried and true
Available to me and you
The road less traveled by
The poet sadly wrote

Leading to that City's lights
Streets of gold, gates of pearl
That righteous place
The prodigal's soul seeks
Where our Father stands and waits
Robe in Hand and feast prepared!

Sites Past

There are sites from our past we think to revisit
Memories of the people we knew come to mind
And when we arrive we sadly find
The site has changed and we are strangers
To those residing there and the scenery changed

We are reminded of an old adage
That one can never go back to relive the past
No matter how hard we might try fast
The people we knew leave like we did
And we realize nothing worldly lasts

A final goodbye in a eulogy spoken
Seeing the memories as gifts in tokens
Life moves on in its approval of renewal
A new day, new vistas filled with new friends
And me realizing my focus on what is ahead

I have progressed from those locations
Growth offered and readily chosen
The unknown before me but directions clear
A promise made by One who does not lie
Follow me to a destination He said that is near

Sometimes, it seems the challenge too great
And the strength of purpose seems not exist
But a resonance of heart urges us on
To a certain place beyond our sight
Established by our God in all that is right!

In Pursuit of Purpose

I have not traveled here before
But I have listened to ancients' lore
And now wondering if it's true
Will this ancient trail take me
From where I am to You.

I am traveling, really, from nothingness
Having heard of a promise made
After You suffered and arose from the dead
You left to prepare a place for us
That where You are we may be too!

I can see the path clearly ahead of me
Leading into the shadows of the trees
I know of no other way ahead
For me to go in this dark day
As I began my pursuit of that promise made!

Sorry friends but I have to leave
The drought here has compelled me go
I hope you will choose to join me now
This place we are in just rubble
Living here now for me a struggle.

Alone, I take my first steps
Following this travel-worn ancient path
Believing what lies ahead far more promising
Than the emptiness I have known
And seek to escape!

When The Roses No Longer Bloom

When the roses no longer bloom
And the sun no longer shines
When the birds no longer sing
And love dies in the gloom

When light turns to darkness
And hope lies in the street
And the only peace is bought with guns
And truth falls at men's feet

And our God abandons the scene
Relief sought but no power to access
Babies carcasses litter the land
And nothing left sacred left stand

Human beings in the wake
Not knowing the sarcophagus prepared
Is for each of them has their name
In the distance a funeral dirge

Like the lemming running to escape
Their drowning in the sea awaits
No one now to point the way
To the higher road that is straight!

Reflections

Reflections from my past
Pictures clear in memory
All are pleasant still
And will always last
Entry to an ancient place
Only Dreamers hope to find
For a moment all is still
Odors rise of woodsmoke and sage
The fires of those gathered here
Drums rise hearts beating in time
Eerie voices singing praise
Slowly now with heads held high
Dancers from the mist arrive
The bells chime with the fall of feet
Old ones, regal as they dance
After them the women inline
Young women with their shawls
Like angels these regal queens
Far off looks borne of reverence clear
The Nations of The Red Race clearly appear
Living The Dream that will never die

This is a photo of me taken in the bush west of Baraga, Michigan, a few years ago. I was unaware of what would develop in my life after a heart attack and further change in how I envisioned things. This book is called poetry, with me not being sure whether it is or not. I have read Chaucer, Frost, Longfellow and so many others, enjoying what they wrote as poetry. So, I guess it is up to the reader to decide what it is or isn't.

Made in the USA
Columbia, SC
01 June 2024